Hoops

BEN KATZ & DEBBIE NYMAN

STECK-VAUGHN
Harcourt Achieve

www.HarcourtAchieve.com

10801 N. Mopac Expressway
Building # 3
Austin, TX 78759
1.800.531.5015

Steck-Vaughn is a trademark of Harcourt Achieve Inc. registered in the United States of America and/or other jurisdictions. All inquiries should be mailed to Harcourt Achieve Inc., P.O. Box 27010, Austin, TX 78755.

www.rubiconpublishing.com

Project Editors: Miriam Bardswich, Kim Koh
Editorial Assistant: Lori McNeelands
Art/Creative Director: Jennifer Drew-Tremblay
Assistant Art Director: Jen Harvey
Designer: Gabriela Castillo

6 7 8 9 10   5 4 3 2 1

Hoops
ISBN 1-41902-401-9

CONTENTS

Title–Getty Images/Photodisc

MORE than a Ball and Hoop

It's a passion —
Dedication, Determination, Domination

It's a calling —
Playing, Playing, Playing

It's a lesson —
Facing Fear … Failure

It's a teacher —
Charm, Change, Challenge

It's a student —
Invent, Improve, Imagine

It's why I can't sleep at night —
Driving, Dunking, Dreaming

It's a rhythm
It's a beat
It's a ball and a hoop.

Domination: *control*

Girl and Boy, Scoreboard–Stock Xchange; Boy With Ball–istockphoto; View From Above–Corbis; Dunking–Corbis; Background–Corbis

PLY FLS

HOOPOLOGY 101

And one: When a player scores a basket and is fouled at the same time. The player then gets a foul shot.

Big man: A tall and strong player who stays close to the basket.

Baller: A basketball player

Drive: To go to the basket while dribbling.

Battle for position: When players do whatever they can to get close to the basket.

Fadeaway: When a player shoots the ball while falling away from the basket.

Beat the defender: When an offensive player is able to drive past the defender who is guarding him.

Foul shot: When a player is fouled while taking a shot, he/she is given a free shot from the foul line.

Dish: When a player drives to the basket and then passes off to a big man.

Outside shot: Taking a shot far away from the rim (usually around the 3-point line).

Rock: The basketball.

Full-court press: When a team closely guards the offensive team along the entire length of the court.

Swat: To block a shot.

Vertical: How high a player can jump.

Handle: A player who can dribble the ball well is said to have a good "handle."

Windmill: A dunk where the player moves his or her arm in a full circle before dunking.

Hops: The ability to jump high.

Zone defense: When each defender is responsible for an area on the court instead of a specific player.

Layup: A shot that is taken very close to the basket.

Loose ball: When the ball is rolling on the court and no one has possession.

360: A dunk where the player spins a full turn in the air before dunking.

Man-to-man: A type of defense in which a defensive player guards the offensive player.

ON THE Court

Trees, Kids in Foreground, Wall–stock Xchange; All Other Images–istockphoto

The Key:

A 19 x 12 foot area that surrounds the basket. Also known as the paint. An offensive player is only allowed to remain in the key for three seconds. When a foul shot is taken, the players line up around the key — ready to get the rebound.

The Foul Line:

The side of the key furthest from the basket is called the foul line. If a player is fouled on a shot, he receives two free shots from the foul line.

The Three-Point Line:

Any shot made from behind the three-point line is worth three points.

Yao's Path to Greatness

warm up

Think about the word "greatness." What does this word mean to you? Who do you think is "great"?

Photographers love him and the fans crowd lines to buy tickets to his games. Drafted by the Houston Rockets in 2002, Yao Ming quickly became a household name.

At 7'6", Yao isn't your average basketball player. Unlike most NBA stars, he was born and raised in China — thousands of miles and 13 time zones away from the NBA.

In this interview with sportswriter Ric Bucher, Yao Ming thinks about straddling two cultures.

drafted: *selected to play in a team*
straddling: *participating in, living in*

FYI

- "Yao" is Yao Ming's surname and "Ming" is his given name. Both of his parents played basketball for China's national teams.
- His father Yao Zhi Yuan is 6'7" and his mother Fang Feng Di is 6'3".

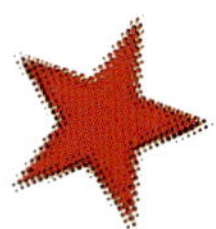

Ric Bucher: Has playing in the US changed your personality?

Yao Ming: It has fertilized my growth as a person. The intense competition of the NBA brings out more emotion in me, and I'm more willing to display that emotion now.

RB: Why did the US basketball team play so badly in the [2004] Olympics?

YM: It's a lack of understanding of international basketball, the rules, the players. Team China has the same problem.

RB: What's the biggest misconception that Americans have about China?

YM: I don't know, but the Chinese seem to know more about Americans than the other way around.

RB: Would you ever want to be a US citizen?

YM: Not right now. … I still feel very Chinese. China is my country. Besides, basketball is an international language.

---

fertilized: *helped*
misconception: *wrong idea*

"The only expectation I have of myself is to play well."

— Yao Ming, October 2002

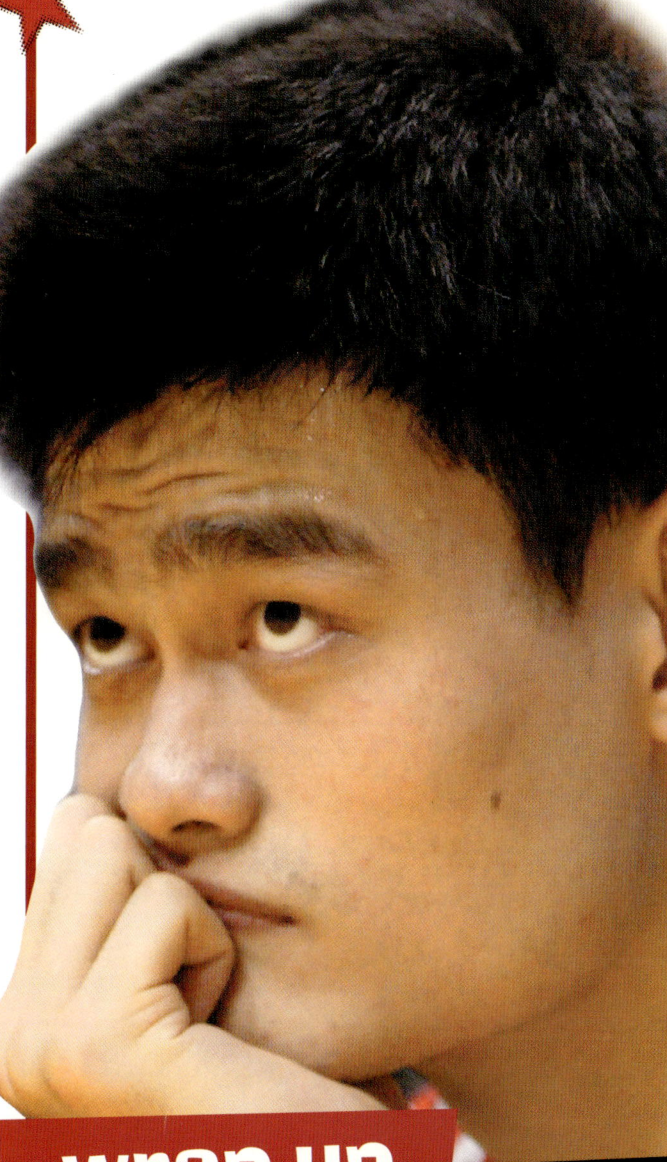

WEB CONNECTIONS

Yi Jianlian is a young player who is NBA bound. Look him up and see if he has joined Yao and the others in the NBA. Create a T-chart to compare Yao Ming's statistics with Yi Jianlian's.

wrap up

1. "Basketball is an international language." Discuss with a partner what Yao Ming means by this statement.
2. Imagine that you are 7'6" and wear size 18 shoes. With a partner, brainstorm all the challenges you would face because of your size. Would being bigger change the way you feel inside?

Illustrated by JEREMY BENNISON

THE NEXT GAME

I'M OPEN! PASS THE BALL!!

FORGET IT! I GOT THE SHOT!

JOSH, YOU'RE SUCH A BALL-HOG. YOU NEVER PASS!

MAYBE I'D PASS IF YOU DIDN'T SUCK ... !

COACH'S CORNER

LATER, AT THE PARK
YO, STEPH, I WONDER WHAT HE WANTS?

CAN I PLAY WITH YOU GUYS?

I'M SORRY I WAS SUCH AN IDIOT. I REALLY LIKE BASKETBALL AND I'D LIKE TO LEARN HOW TO PLAY BETTER.

IT TURNS OUT THAT PLAYING BASKETBALL IS A GOOD WAY TO MAKE NEW FRIENDS ...

COACH'S CORNER
YOUR TEACHER SAYS YOU'RE BACK ON TRACK WITH YOUR HOMEWORK, JERMAINE. WELCOME BACK TO THE TEAM. ... THANKS FOR FILLING IN, JOSH ...
IF IT'S OK WITH YOU, I THINK JOSH SHOULD STAY ON THE TEAM. ***HE'S A GOOD PLAYER!***

wrap up

1. Why do you think players who are still in school need to keep up their grades to play on a team? Do you think this is a fair rule? Discuss your opinion with a partner.
2. In the story Josh says, "I was just helping out my teammates." Make a list of all the ways a player can help out other players both on and off the court.

Up Close and Personal with

a Real Champion

warm up

Imagine throwing or dribbling a basketball while seated in a wheelchair. What would you have to do differently? Share your thoughts with the class.

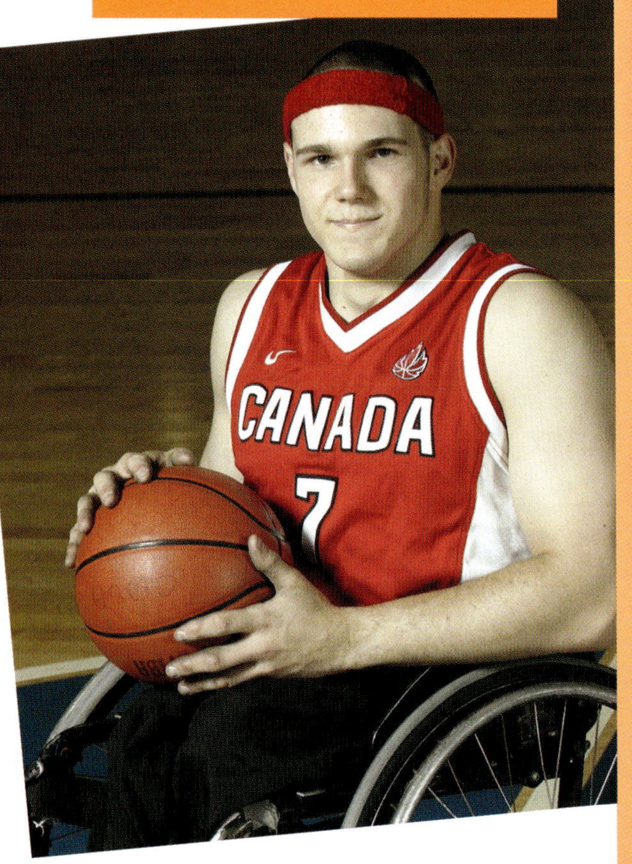

Brad Bowden Photograph courtesy of the Canadian Wheelchair Basketball Association

FYI

The Canadian Men's Wheelchair Basketball Team won the gold medal at the 2004 Paralympic Games.

The Canadian Women's Wheelchair Basketball Team won the bronze medal.

Bradley Bowden is a member of the Canadian National Wheelchair Basketball Team. He has played on the team since 2003. Before joining the team, Bradley played at the provincial level where he won a number of championships. BOLDPRINT interviewed this amazing baller.

BOLDPRINT: How did you get involved in wheelchair basketball?

Bradley Bowden: As a kid growing up I didn't even know that wheelchair sports existed. When I was 13 or 14 my grandparents took me to a wheelchair league. I started playing once a week. Eventually, I made an All-Star team. I did well there and was voted team Rookie of the Year. I received a real basketball wheelchair, which meant I could try out for some traveling teams.

BP: Did you play other sports before basketball?

BB: Actually, before I made the National Basketball Team in 2003, I was on the National Sledge Hockey Team. I played sledge hockey in the winter 1998 and 2002 Paralympics.

Sledge Hockey: *players sit on boards set on runners or long skate blades*

BP: What are some of the differences between basketball and wheelchair basketball?

BB: Both are pretty much the same except for a couple of rules that are adapted from stand up. For example, "traveling" in wheelchair basketball is when a player takes more then two pushes of his wheels without dribbling.

BP: What is a typical day like in the life of Bradley Bowden?

BB: Since we are training for the Paralympics right now I work out everyday, twice a day. I get up at 9:30 AM and meet up with my teammates for a workout. Some days we do chair skills, such as towing other people, to improve strength and speed. Other days we do shooting drills and other basketball related things. Then I go home to eat and relax. After that, it's back to the gym for evening scrimmages.

BP: Do you have any words of advice for young athletes?

BB: Try everything! My grandparents had to drag me to my first basketball practice and now they can't drag me off the court! Also, always try your best and have fun. If you are not having fun, try something else ... just get out there and play!

---

adapted: *changed*
scrimmages: *practice games*

wrap up

1. List the skills that a wheelchair basketball player needs to develop to become a strong player.
2. Imagine that you are a sports announcer. Write the script for a play-by-play in a wheelchair basketball game. Read your script aloud to a partner in the voice of an announcer.

WEB CONNECTIONS

On the Internet, enter "**wheel-chair basketball**" into a search engine. Using the information you find, create a pamphlet about the game. Write the instructions on how to play the game, and list the rules.

Changing Gear

warm up

Look around you — what types of clothes are people wearing? Do you notice a certain style of clothing or hairstyle that a lot of people have?

The 50s and 60s

Bob Cousy
Pro Career
1950–1963

Hair: Brushcut
Jersey: Tight-fitting, plain jersey
Shorts: Shorts stopped at the upper thigh.
Socks: Socks were pulled up to the mid-calf.
Shoes: Low-cut canvas shoes were in fashion.
Accessories: Some players also wore a belt.

The 70s and 80s

Julius "Dr. J" Erving
Pro Career
1971–1987

Hair: Afro
Jersey: Tight jersey with a flashy design.
Short: Shorts stopped at upper thigh.
Socks: Socks had colorful stripes and were pulled up to the mid-calf.
Shoes: High-cut leather shoes were popular.
Accessories: Some players wore thick sweatbands on their wrists.

Bob Cousy Photograph Courtesy of the Boston Celtics; Julius Erving–Bettmann/CORBIS/MAGMA; Allen Iverson–CP/ Michael Kolvenbach; Michael Jordan–Bob Leverone/TSN/ZUMA Press/KEYSTONE Press

The 80s and 90s

Hair: Bald
Jersey: Loose-fitting jersey
Shorts: Shorts went to just above the knee. Some players wore spandex shorts underneath their uniform shorts.
Socks: Socks were white and low-cut.
Shoes: High-cut Air Jordans

Today

Hair: Cornrows
Jersey: Extra baggy
Shorts: Shorts go to below the knees and are very baggy.
Socks: Ankle height
Shoes: Shoes are mid-cut with loose laces.
Accessories: Headband, arm sleeves, elastic band on wrist, tattoos

wrap up

1. If you could step into the gear of one of the players, who would you choose? Explain why you chose this gear.
2. With a partner design the gear for the basketball player of the future. Draw a design for the uniform, shoes, and hairstyle. Compare your design with your classmates.

MVP Lauren Jackson

warm up

What do you think it takes to be a world champion in a sport?

Lauren Jackson was born in Australia on May 11, 1981. When she was just two weeks old, she began traveling with her parents while they played basketball on the men's and women's Australian National Teams. It was no surprise to anyone when Lauren began playing ball at four years old.

Today, Lauren Jackson is considered the best female "basketballer" in the world.

Lauren's coaches say she is successful because she works hard and is determined to succeed.

When Lauren was 12 years old, her parents told her that whatever she did, she had to strive to be the best she could be. Lauren decided then that she would play in the 2000 Olympic Games in Sydney. Lauren worked hard, developed her game, and accomplished her goal. She won a silver medal in Sydney and went on to win another silver medal in the 2004 Olympics in Greece.

Her next goal is to win an Olympic gold medal in Beijing. Will she achieve her goal? We will have to wait and see.

Lauren Jackson–Mitchell Layton/NewSport/Corbis/MAGMA; Stadium, Basketball–istockphoto; Trophy–Corbis/CB025525

ACCOMPLISHMENTS

1991 At the age of 10, voted MVP at the under-12 Australian state championship.

1996 At 15 years old, invited to play at the Australian Institute of Sport in Canberra.

2000 Won a silver medal at the Sydney Olympics.

2001 Number one WNBA draft choice of the Seattle Storm.

2003 Named WNBA MVP of the Year.

2003 Broke the WNBA scoring record on June 8 in a game against Los Angeles.

2004 Won a silver medal at the Olympics in Greece.

FYI

When Lauren began playing with the Seattle Storm, she chose jersey number 15 in honor of her mother who also wore that number.

wrap up

1. Using the information from this article, write a short speech you would use to introduce Lauren Jackson to her fans.
2. Lauren Jackson left her country and family to play basketball in the US. In Lauren's voice, write a journal entry describing some difficulties or challenges she faced, and some of the rewards she experienced.

WEB CONNECTIONS

Lauren Jackson plays basketball in Australia and the US. Use the Internet to find other players who have come from other countries to play in the NBA or WNBA. Organize the information in a chart.

AIR JORDAN 23

warm up

Think of some people who are the best in their fields – the best actors, rap artists, tennis players etc. What is it that makes these people the best? Share your answers in a small group.

"I can accept failure, but I can't accept not trying."

— Michael Jordan

Jordan–Simon Bruty/SI/NewSport/Corbis/MAGMA; Stadium–stock Xchange

Michael Jordan. Everyone knows the name. Air Jordan. Number 23. Flying through the air, tongue wagging, scoring points, playing defense — he did it all. He holds six NBA championships, countless MVP awards, and more records than anyone can name. He is the best basketball player of all time, and maybe the greatest athlete to ever play team sports.

Basketball wasn't always easy for Michael though. In grade ten, he was cut from his high school varsity team. It drove him to work harder. He practiced so much over the summer that the next year he was one of the best players in the entire state of North Carolina.

In 1982, Michael went on to play college basketball for the University of North Carolina. As a freshman, he drained a 15-foot jump shot that won his team the NCAA Championship. It was a dramatic shot that made him famous. But it wouldn't be his last.

Two years later, Michael burst onto the NBA as an explosive, high-flying rookie. Air Jordan was born. During his incredible NBA career, Michael accomplished just about everything you possibly can in the sport of basketball. He even found time to win two Olympic gold medals, star in a few movies, develop his own line of athletic gear, and take a crack at professional baseball.

Many people ask, what made Michael Jordan so great? The answer is simple — passion.

---

freshman: *first-year college student*

Passion for the sport, passion for succeeding, and a passion for his fans. It is passion that drove him to work harder than any other player in the game. It is passion that elevated his game beyond the ordinary. No matter how good people said Michael Jordan was, when you watched him play, he was always better.

In a meaningless regular season game in the middle of February, Michael Jordan would play his heart out because he knew that somewhere in the stands there might be a family that had saved all their money to come and watch him play just once — and he didn't want to disappoint them. That's the kind of player he was.

As Michael himself once said,

"I've always believed that if you put in the work, the results will come. I don't do things half-heartedly. Because I know if I do, then I can expect half-hearted results."

---

elevated: *raised*

FYI

- Named the century's greatest athlete, but he can't swim or ice skate.
- Played in 1,072 games, which equals 41,011 minutes.
- Finished his career with 32,292 points, 5,633 assists, and 6,672 rebounds.
- Wore his North Carolina college shorts under his Chicago Bulls uniform in every professional game he played.

Jersey Courtesy of The Jersey Source; Micheal Jordan–CP/Kathy Willens; Stadium–stock Xchange

Michael Jordan always put in the work, and the results speak for themselves.

NBA All–Defensive First Team:

1988, 89, 90 ,91, 92, 93, 96, 97, 98

NBA World Champion:

1991, 92, 93, 96, 97, 98

NBA MVP:

1988, 91, 92, 96, 98

NBA Rookie of the Year:

1991, 92, 93, 96, 97, 98

NBA Finals MVP:

1991, 92, 93, 96, 97, 98

NBA All–Rookie Team:

1991, 92, 93, 96, 97, 98

All–NBA First Team:

1987, 88, 89, 90, 91, 92, 93, 96, 97, 98

All–NBA First Team:

1987, 88, 89, 90, 91, 92, 93, 96, 97, 98

NBA Slam Dunk Champion:

1987, 88

wrap up

1. With a partner, discuss Michael Jordan's statement on page 22. Name people you know who have shown the same attitude.
2. Write an email to a friend explaining why you think Michael Jordan is a hero.

WEB CONNECTIONS

Using the Internet, find out more about Michael Jordan's career. Did he set or break any records in the NBA? Did any other players ever play beyond 40 years of age? Using the information, create a trading card about Jordan.

The Tall and the Short of it

warm up

Imagine that you wake up one morning a foot or two taller than you are now. How do you think your life would change?

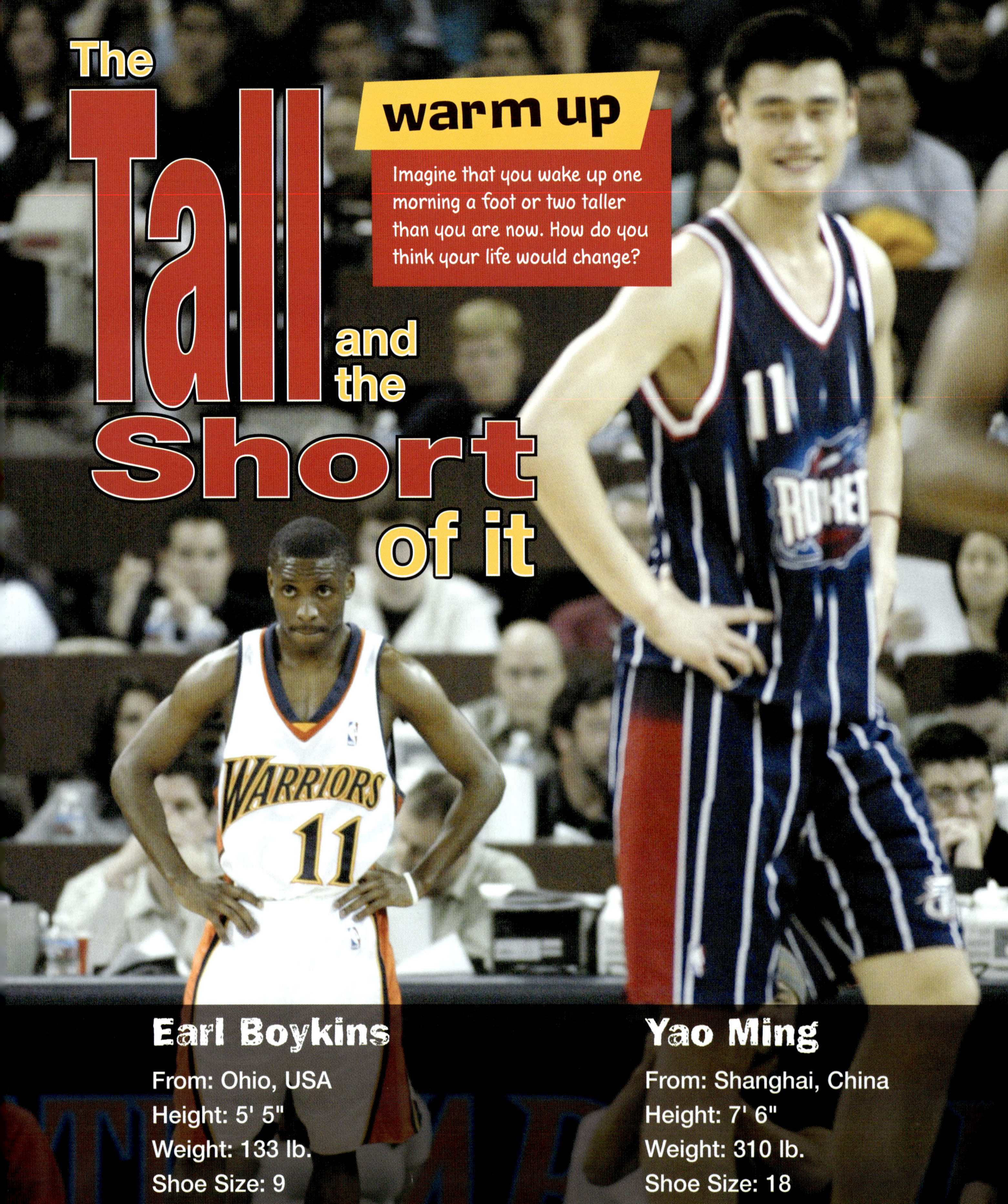

Earl Boykins

From: Ohio, USA
Height: 5' 5"
Weight: 133 lb.
Shoe Size: 9
Earl is the smallest man in the NBA, however, he is one of the strongest. He uses his speed and strength to cause trouble for taller players trying to guard him.

Yao Ming

From: Shanghai, China
Height: 7' 6"
Weight: 310 lb.
Shoe Size: 18
For a man his size, he has a soft touch and the skill to make shots around the basket.

Margo Dydek

From: Warsaw, Poland
Height: 7' 2"
Weight: 223 lb.
Shoe Size: 13
Margo, as she is known, is believed to be the tallest woman alive making her athletic ability even more amazing.

Shannon Johnson

From: South Carolina, USA
Height: 5' 7"
Weight: 152 lb.
Shoe Size: 8
Despite her height, Shannon is a constant All Star and won a gold medal in the 2004 Olympics.

wrap up

1. Imagine that you have the chance to interview a giant of the court. List five questions you would ask the person.
2. If you had your choice of height or skill, which would you choose? Explain your choice.

WEB CONNECTIONS

Using the Internet, find out the tallest and shortest players to ever play in the NBA, then draw them to scale.

BIG Foot

This is the actual size of

FYI

Shaq is 7' 1", weighs 325 lb., and wears a size 22 shoe.

Shaq often donates shoes to charity events and auctions.

He has also sent shoes to young players who cannot afford to buy custom-made shoes.

Shaquille O'Neal's shoe.

Dunking!

warm up

Which moments or plays in football, tennis, baseball or skateboarding bring crowds to their feet? What makes these moments so entertaining for the crowds?

Vince Carter

Carter is known for his power. When he throws down a dunk, it looks like the rim is hanging on for dear life. Carter is also known for his explosive vertical jumps of over 40 inches — that's over three feet!

Michael Jordan

Michael Jordan's nickname was "Air Jordan" because he looked like he was floating through air when he dunked. During games Michael would jump for a shot … wait for everyone else to come down … and then toss the ball into the hoop.

Michael Jordan Photo by NBA Entertainment/ZUMA Press/KEYSTONE Press

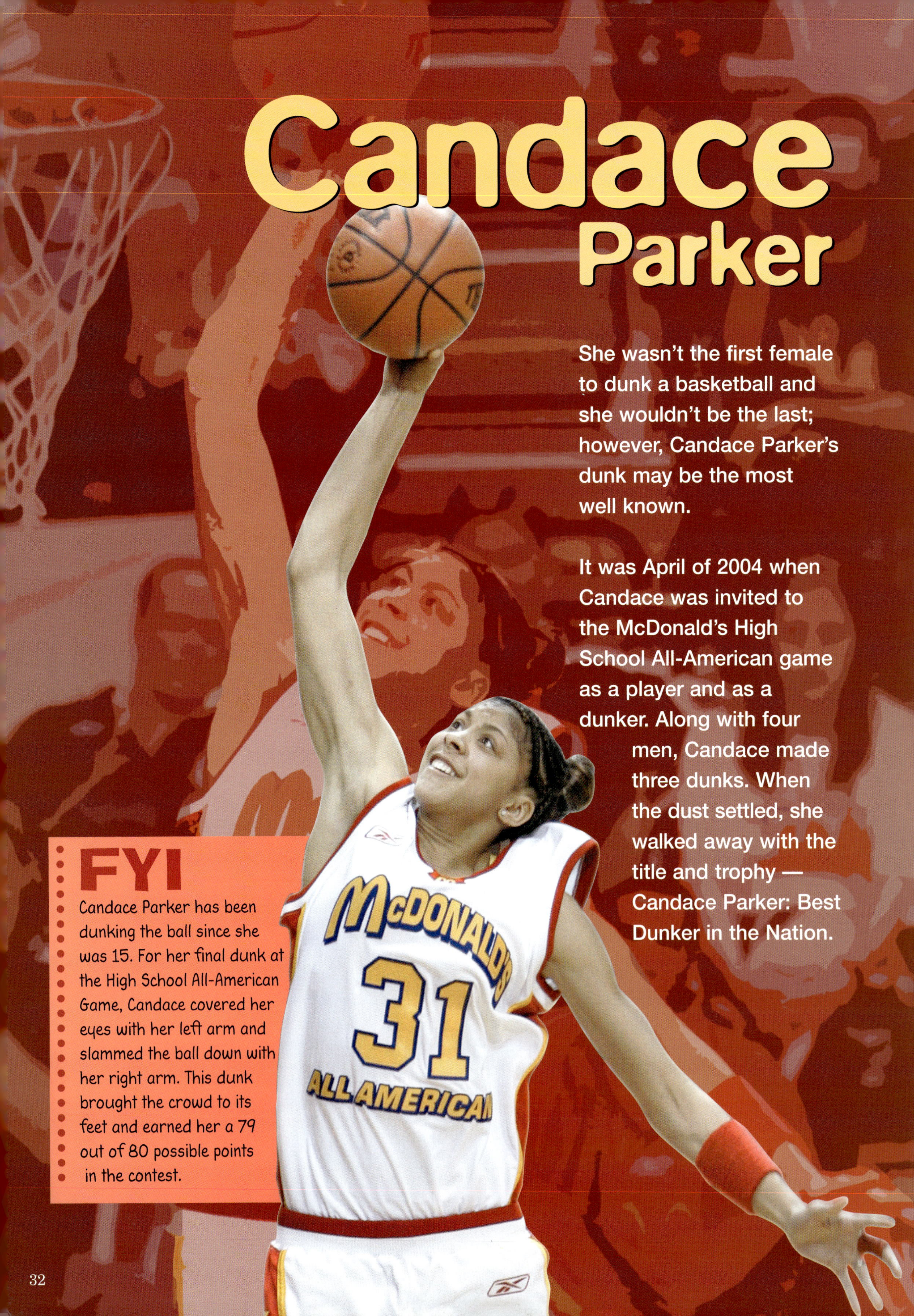

Candace Parker

She wasn't the first female to dunk a basketball and she wouldn't be the last; however, Candace Parker's dunk may be the most well known.

It was April of 2004 when Candace was invited to the McDonald's High School All-American game as a player and as a dunker. Along with four men, Candace made three dunks. When the dust settled, she walked away with the title and trophy — Candace Parker: Best Dunker in the Nation.

FYI

Candace Parker has been dunking the ball since she was 15. For her final dunk at the High School All-American Game, Candace covered her eyes with her left arm and slammed the ball down with her right arm. This dunk brought the crowd to its feet and earned her a 79 out of 80 possible points in the contest.

Lisa Leslie

Lisa Leslie made history when she put down a simple one-handed dunk on an easy breakaway. She is not the tallest player or the fastest, but she was the first woman to ever dunk in the WNBA.

wrap up

1. Brainstorm a list of adjectives to describe the "dunk" in basketball. Select words from the article to add to your list.
2. Share your list of adjectives with a partner. Together write a poem to capture the excitement of the "dunk" in a game. You might want to repeat some words or use rhyming words. Give your poem a title.

Lisa Leslie–Lori Conn/ZUMA Press/KEYSTONE Press

Game Day RI

warm up

A ritual is a repeated act or series of acts. Do you have any rituals that you follow in the morning, before you go to bed, or before a test? For example, do you have a lucky shirt that you like to wear for important events or tests?

I take a nap and listen to Caribbean music to get my energy flowing.

— Adonal Foyle, Golden State Warriors

Kevin Garnett fills his hands with chalk. He rubs it in a little and then tosses the rest in a puff of dust at the media. This is a tribute to Michael Jordan, who did almost exactly the same thing.

My ritual on game day is to eat a turkey club sandwich on whole wheat toast with mayo and swiss. I eat chips, a little pasta salad, and take a nap before I leave for the game. Right when I wake up, before I leave the hotel, I eat a plate of fruit with a pitcher of iced tea.

— Tyrone Hill, Miami Heat

Girl–Getty Images/PhotoDisc/AA050205; Arm With Ball–Getty Images/PhotoDisc/SP000863

---

tribute: *act of respect*

TUALS

I really don't have any rituals that I go through every game. Some rituals work one day and the next day they don't! The most important thing for me is to get my mind focused on whatever my role is going to be for that game!

— Margo Dydek, San Antonio Silver Stars

I pray during the national anthem and I chest bump Amy Fieck really hard during starting line-ups.

— Natalie Yudt, University of Wisconsin

Wisconsin University Badgers forward Ray Nixon will only tie his shoes during a specific pre-game stretch, and then he only uses a double knot.

— Wisconsin University Badgers

Basically, I go to the morning shoot around, I go home, have some lunch, then I take a long bath and get ready to come to the gym. I need to have my headbands and wristbands too. Without them, I'm lost.

— Andrea Stinson, Detroit Shock

wrap up

1. In a small group, create your own rituals page similar to this.
2. Does your school have any rituals that are repeated to celebrate certain holidays or special events? Choose one ritual that you participate in at school and write a brief description of the ritual.

WEB CONNECTIONS

Research a favorite celebrity to find out if this celebrity has any rituals. Share your information with the class.

The Canadian

warm up

Has anyone ever judged you unfairly? How did it make you feel?

The Canadian Half Pints are a basketball team. All of the players are Little People.

One day Phil Watson challenged his friend Mr. T. to a basketball game. Phil was sure he would win because he was so much taller than Mr. T.

Phil was in for a big shock. Not only was Mr. T. in great shape, he was also fast and skilled on the basketball court.

CHECKPOINT
What can you learn from Phil Watson's mistake?

Phil was beaten three times in a row. Playing with Mr. T. gave Phil the idea to create a basketball team of Little People. This is how the Canadian Half Pints was formed.

The average height of a Half Pints player is 4'3". The players are between 17 and 34 years old.

The team has played during half-time breaks against NBA players; however, the team's main job is to visit schools all over North America.

The players demonstrate their amazing basketball skills, and they pass on an important message: Do not judge or tease people just because they look different. Make a friend instead.

FYI

- The Half Pints have played 3,206 basketball games. They have only lost 11. Wow!
- "Dwarfism" is a medical condition. The correct name for someone with this condition is "Little Person."
- A Little Person can grow to a height of 4'10" or less.
- Dwarfism affects 1 in every 7,000 to 10,000 people.

Half Pints

The "Don't Tease Program" has three important points:

1. Friendship — Make new friends no matter what they look like.

2. Reach for that Dream — It is important to believe in yourself no matter what you look like. Everyone has a talent to be discovered.

3. Listen and Learn — Listen to your parents, coaches, and teachers. If you listen, you will learn and improve.

The Half Pints talk about these ideas while crushing the school's basketball team.

Phil Watson said that one of the nicest comments he ever received about the Half Pints was: "Physically, I'm still looking down at them. But after the show, I'm looking up at them."

CHECKPOINT

What do you think the person who said this meant?

wrap up

1. Bullying is a very serious issue. Work with a friend to make a list of suggestions that you think would help to stop bullying.
2. Write three questions that you would ask a Half Pints player.

WEB CONNECTIONS

Imagine you have been hired by the Half Pints to design a new logo for their team. Visit this website to come up with some ideas: **www.canadianhalfpints.com.** Display your logos in the classroom.

Hook

warm up

As a class, discuss stories you know or have read about people who have turned their lives around. How did they do this?

CHECKPOINT

Why do you think certain names from this quote are written in square brackets?

FYI

Since his release from prison, Hook has started a group called Project Straight Path. This project helps kids who are facing the same problems he faced as a child.

Demetrius "Hook" Mitchell was best known for jumping over cars, tables, and even people to slam dunk a basketball. At only 5'9", Hook was a street-ball legend.

When he was young, Hook could jump higher, run faster, and play the game of basketball better than anyone he grew up with.

NBA superstar and childhood friend, Gary Payton, said, "[Hook] was better than me, he was better than Jason [Kidd], Antonio [Davis], he was better than everybody."

As a teenager, Hook used to win money in dunk contests against older college players. He could do any dunk that NBA players do today.

However, when Hook's childhood friends, Gary Payton, Jason Kidd, and Antonio Davis all went on to the NBA ... Hook went to jail.

Basketball Player Drawing–istockphoto; All other images–Kicked Down Productions

. . . a Street-ball Legend

Hook made all the wrong choices. He hung out with the wrong people, got involved in drugs, and didn't focus on school.

One day Hook walked into a video store. He put his hand into the shape of a gun inside his jacket. Then he ordered the clerk to give him all the money in the register — Hook was high on drugs. He was arrested and given a ten-year sentence.

Today Hook has turned his life around. In jail he matured and educated himself. He studied religion and became a devout Muslim.

"I have only myself to blame for what happened. I made one bad choice after another. I can't shift the blame to other people or my environment. I could have shifted that bad energy into something positive, now I'm doing that."

devout: *serious*
positive: *good*

wrap up

Imagine you have a good friend who is beginning to make poor choices about friends, activities, or school. Write a short note to your friend explaining why you are worried about him or her.

WEB CONNECTIONS

With a partner, visit the website: **www.hookmitchell.com**. Click on "Project Straight Path," and read the description. Present a two-minute oral report to the class, explaining why it is important to make good choices when you're young.

HOOP CITY

In this excerpt from *Hoop City* by Scott Blumenthal and Brett Hodus, a young boy challenges a bully to a game of one-on-one ...

warm up

Have you ever challenged an older friend or sibling to a game that you liked to play? Why do you think it feels so good to play well against them?

I wiped some blood from my lower lip and yelled, "Hey, Jason!" He turned and faced me, "What? You want some more of that, Shorty?" The answer was no. I definitely didn't want any more of that, but a fire was burning inside me.

"You and me, one-on-one." I spoke before I fully thought about this proposition. Playing one-on-one against a player five inches taller, and four years older than me probably wasn't a good idea.

---

proposition: *offer or proposal*

Silhouettes–istockphoto; All Other Images–stockXchange

"What'd you just ask me?" Jason and his friends started laughing. Once again, I was the butt of their jokes. He casually sat down on a bench and sipped from his water bottle. "Go home, Shorty." He wasn't taking me seriously. No one was.

"Or are you just a punk?"

"Stand up and play me one-on-one to 11, Jason." I spit blood onto the ground. "Or are you just a punk?" Everyone who was at the park that day moved in a little bit closer. …

The court began to clear as Jason took off his shirt and revealed an upper body that was twice the size of my own. I took my shirt off in response. It was not a pretty sight. My ribs stuck out, my arms were puny, and I don't think I could have intimidated a beanstalk. I stood there shirtless anyway.

CHECKPOINT
Notice how "Shorty" thinks of himself.

Jason walked toward me and threw the ball hard at my chest. "Check it up, punk!" …

CHECKPOINT
What does Jason think of "Shorty" at this point?

Jason stood in front of me in a weak defensive stance. He wasn't taking me and my 12-year-old body seriously. On the first play I blew past him left, making an easy layup. Jason obviously wasn't too rattled, because on my next possession, his long arm swatted my shot routinely. He regained control of the loose ball and stood at the top of the key, talking trash, "Here it comes. Get ready." …

---

intimidated: *frightened, upset*
routinely: *regularly*

CHECKPOINT
Notice how "Shorty" plans his defense tactics.

I crouched down, getting set defensively. Many defenders like to watch the path of the ball, others like to look into their opponent's eyes. I stared at the hips. I learned that an offensive player wasn't going anywhere unless his hips shifted first. If Jason decided to move, I would know exactly where he was going before his feet did.

As Jason began to yo-yo the ball up and down with his right hand, he noticed my unorthodox defensive style and thought he had the perfect opportunity to open his mouth again. "Any of you guys have a spatula? I think Shorty's stuck to the —" Just as he was about to complete his insult, I sprouted out of my stance, knocking the ball away. I made another uncontested layup, showboating this time with a pretty finger roll. All of Jason's friends started jeering at him as I dribbled back to the top of the key. He'd been embarrassed on the court he used to own. … His nostrils were flaring and beads of sweat dripped down his face. He charged, and began hand checking me with the force of a grizzly bear. I turned my back to him and was pelted by slaps on my wrists and forearms. A voice rang out from the crowd, "Hey, he's foulin' the kid! Play like a man, Helms!"

CHECKPOINT
What do you think the author means by "showboating"?

CHECKPOINT
Notice the author's description of Jason. What does it make you think of?

Despite the harassment, Jason wouldn't let up. He was smacking and pushing with all

---

unorthodox: *unusual*
uncontested: *unchallenged*
harassment: *pestering, annoyance*

Boys on Bench–stockXchange; Silhouette–iStockphoto

his force. I could only get knocked around for so long before I lost control of the ball. I had to do something. …

Shorty's Turn

I noticed Jason's legs were spread wide while he smacked and hacked at the backs of my arms. … I turned around and bounced the ball directly between his open legs. Then I darted past as he lunged for the rock. "Too late!" I exclaimed, grabbing the ball after two bounces and rolling in another layup.

Jason's crew began to razz him even more, "Shorty's making you look stupid, Jay." …

A few of Jason's friends started cheering for me as well. "You're the man, Shorty! Show him what's up!" …

The score went back and forth for the next ten minutes. This was turning into a battle: my quickness against his size, his experience versus my youth, and his pride versus my will.

"… his pride versus my will."

We were tied at ten in a game to eleven. Jason held the ball at the top of the key. Through heavy breaths he muttered, "Next hoop wins." I tried to keep my defensive intensity high, but my tired legs wouldn't cooperate.

CHECKPOINT
Predict what will happen next.

> "Jason turned his back to the basket and powered me deep into the post."

Jason turned his back to the basket and powered me deep into the post.

I leaned my forearm into the middle of his back, desperately trying to hold my ground. I couldn't afford to let him move in any closer. But my last gasp was useless. …

He pumped his fist in the air victoriously and pulled on his shorts in exhaustion. I knew that when this game started he would never have imagined getting that fired up after beating a twelve-year-old kid by a single point. …

CHECKPOINT
Why is this a turning point for Tony?

Jason came over to me and shook my hand with a smile on his face. "Nice game, Tony." I couldn't believe it! He called me Tony.

After that game I was always Tony. I had graduated; no one ever called me Shorty again. I had earned Jason's respect. I could see it in his face when he approached me, and felt it in the firmness of his handshake. He spoke to me before exiting through a hole in the fence. "You've got a ton of game, Tony. If you ever need someone to run with, come up to the Jungle. I'll play with you anytime."

I nodded my head, exhausted and beaten, but respected.

To find out what happens to Tony, pick up a copy of *Hoop City* at the library or local bookstore.
You can also visit **www.scobre.com**.

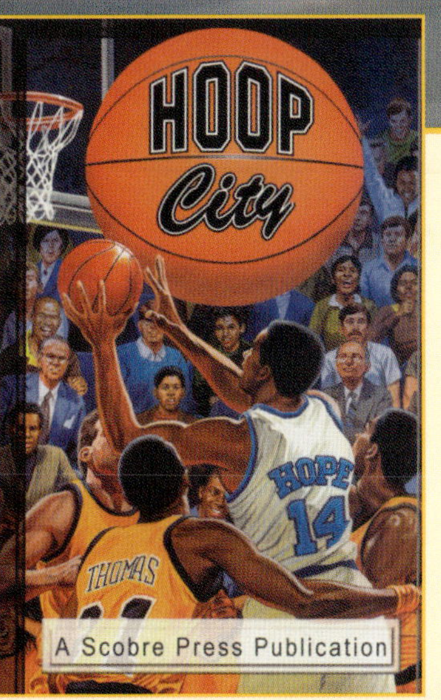

wrap up

1. Do you think Tony made the right decision to challenge Jason to a game of one-on-one? Explain your reasons to a partner. Did you both agree?

2. Read the "three important points" of the Don't Tease Program on page 37. Discuss with a partner how the three points relate to Tony and Jason.

3. "Tony lost the game but finished up a winner." Explain this in a short paragraph.

BASKET

warm up

Interview three people in your class to find out why they love either "playing" or "watching" basketball. Why do you love the game?

Ball is my life. I swear if I never had a basketball I'd be doing nothing with my life. I work harder than anybody else in every part of my game, my shot is sick, my handles are disgusting, and I can jump out of the gym!! I won't stop working until I become one of the best players to come out of Canada. Right now I'm aiming to get a scholarship and hopefully go on to play professional.

— Ashton Smith

I love basketball because it is a fun sport which requires determination and confidence.

— Theodore Rouvas

Basketball is so challenging.

— Adrian Iacovino

I'm always willing to take on a challenge. I'm just a regular baller. But I didn't start out as one. A lot of hard practice and determination is all it took. Beating the best makes you better than the rest. That's how I got game.

— Adlet Gemelus

The court is my second home.

— Lisa Kricfalusi

wrap up

1. The quotations on these pages are from young basketball players. Using no more than 10 words, add your own quote.
2. Using one of the quotations, create a poster to convince other people that basketball is a great game.

ACKNOWLEDGMENTS

The publisher gratefully acknowledges the following for permission to reproduce copyrighted material in this book.

Every reasonable effort has been made to trace the owners of copyrighted material and to make due acknowledgment. Any errors or omissions drawn to our attention will be gladly rectified in future editions.